T H E   C I T Y

SCHOCKEN HAS ALSO PUBLISHED
FRANS MASEREEL'S *LANDSCAPES AND VOICES*,
AND HIS BOOKS *THE SUN* AND *HAMBURG*
ARE FORTHCOMING IN 1989.

FRANS

THE CITY

MASEREEL

SCHOCKEN BOOKS

NEW YORK

First Schocken Books Edition

All rights reserved under International and Pan-American Copyright
Conventions. Published in the United States by Schocken Books
Inc., New York. Distributed by Pantheon Books, a division of
Random House, Inc., New York. Originally published in Germany as
Die Stadt in 1925 by Kurt Wolff Verlag AG, Munich.

Published by arrangement with Stiftung Studienbibliothek zur
Geschichte der Arbeiterbewegung, Zurich.

Library of Congress Cataloging-in-Publication Data
Masereel, Frans, 1889-1972.
The city.
Translation of: Die Stadt.
München : K. Wolff, 1925.
1. Masereel, Frans, 1889-1972.   2. Cities and towns in art.
I. Title.
NE1155.5.M3A4   1988b   769.92′4   88-42769
ISBN 0-8052-0902-6

Manufactured in the United States of America

T H E   C I T Y

"This is the city and I am one of the citizens,
Whatever interests the rest interests me…."
— Walt Whitman

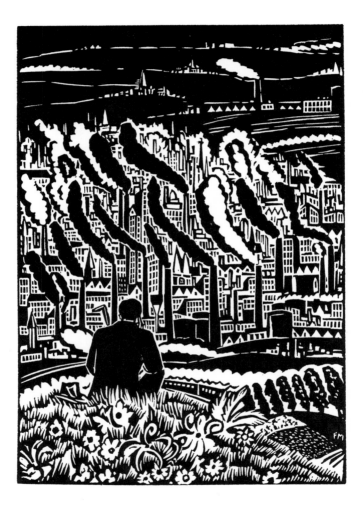

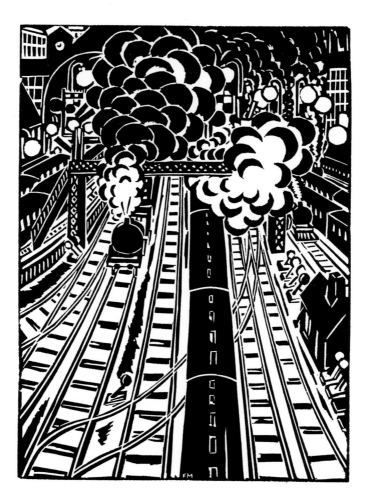

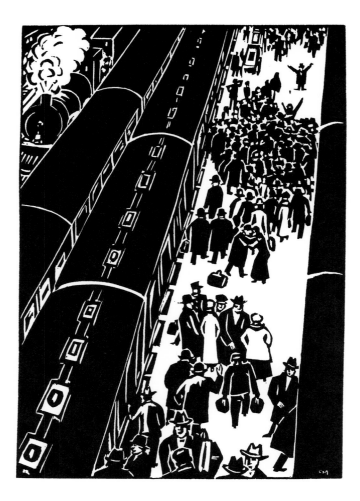

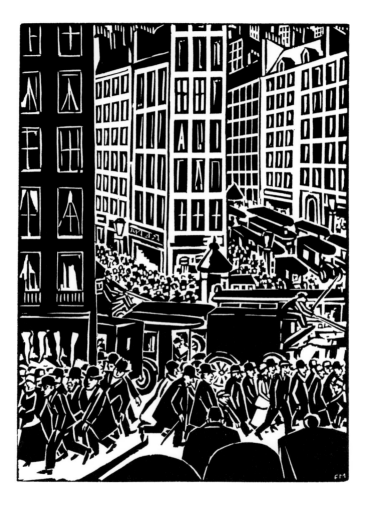

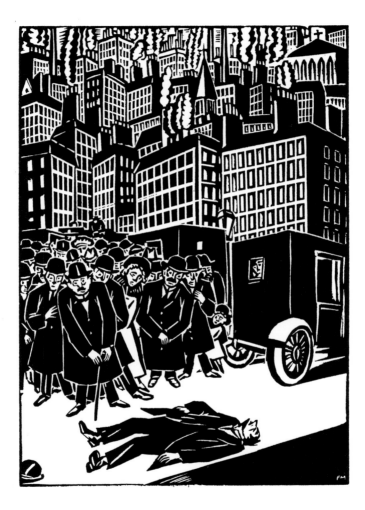

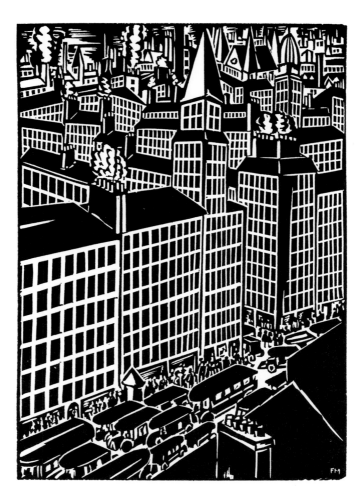

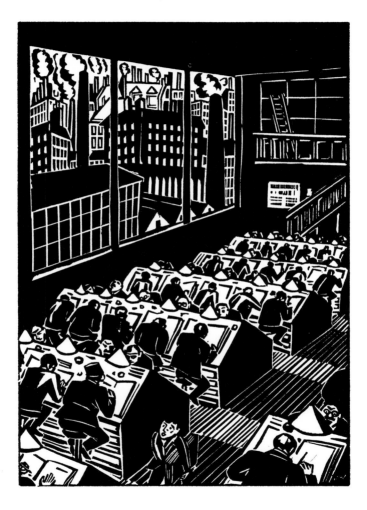

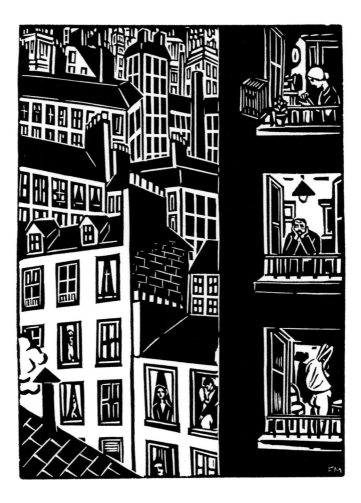

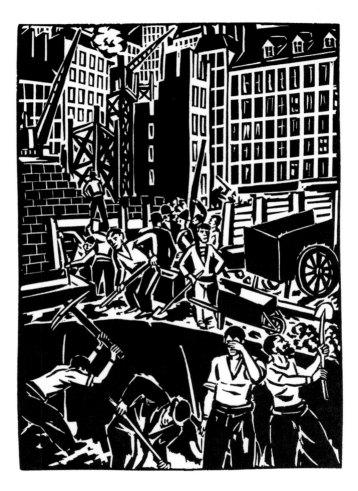

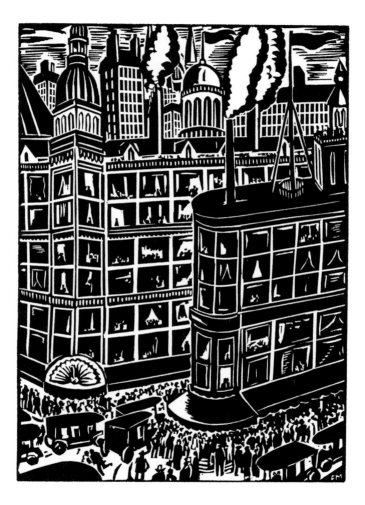

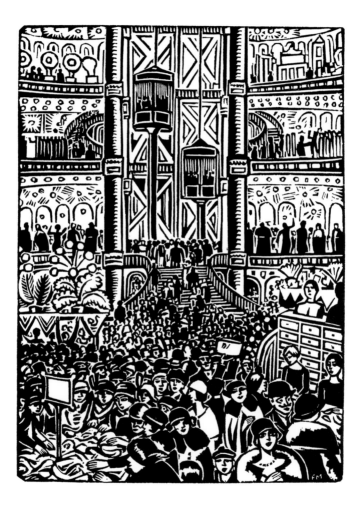

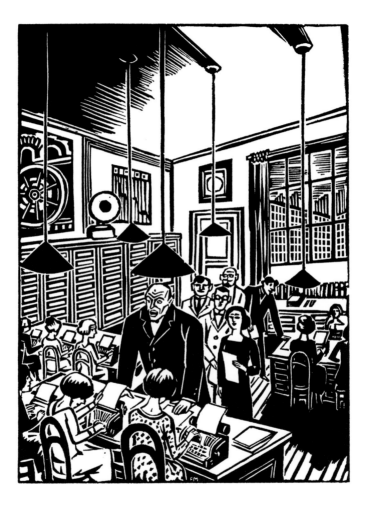

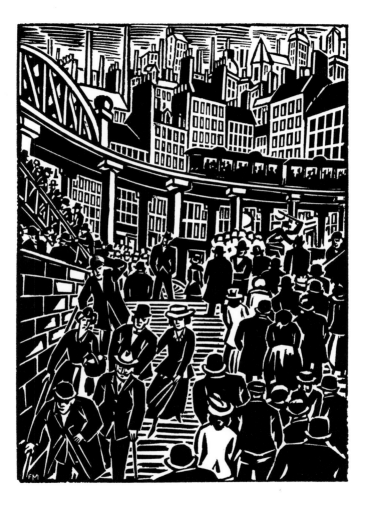

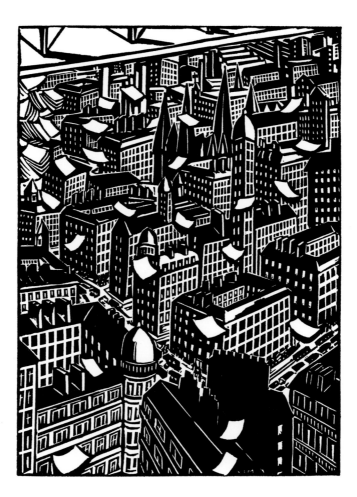

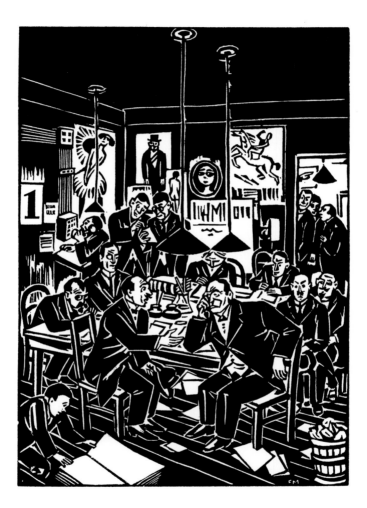

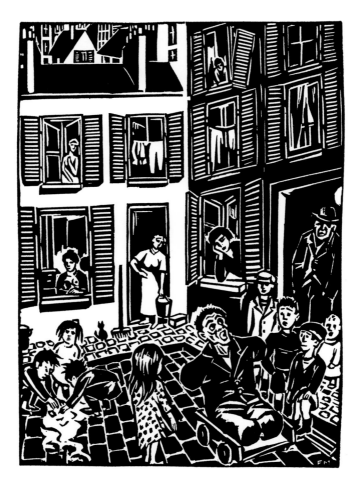

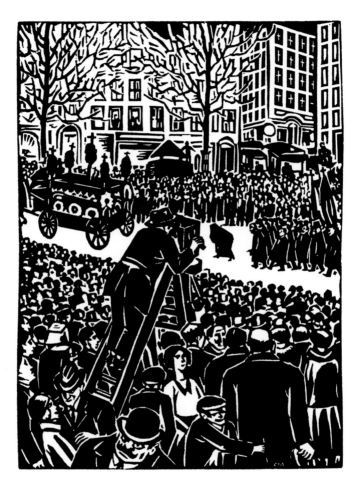

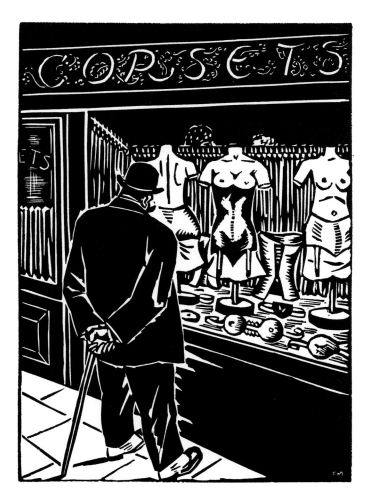

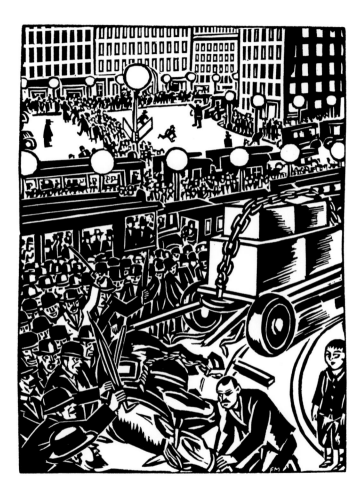

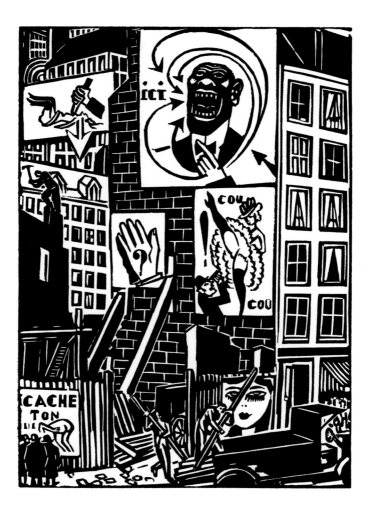

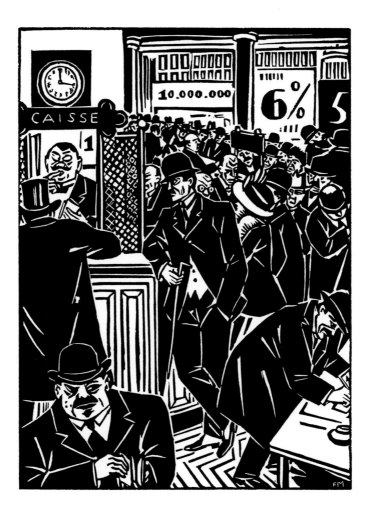

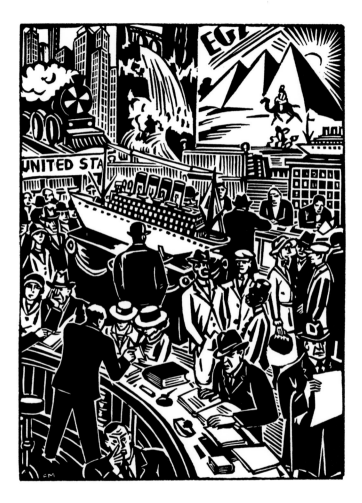

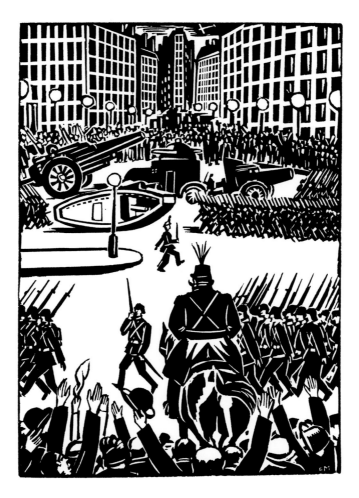

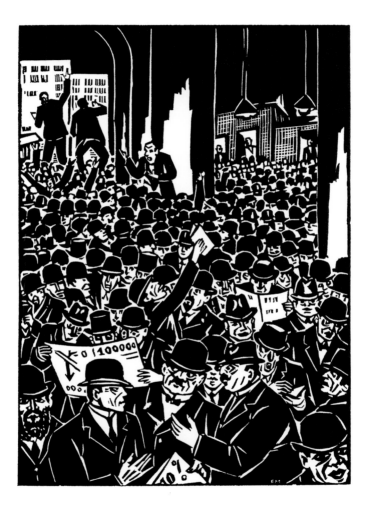

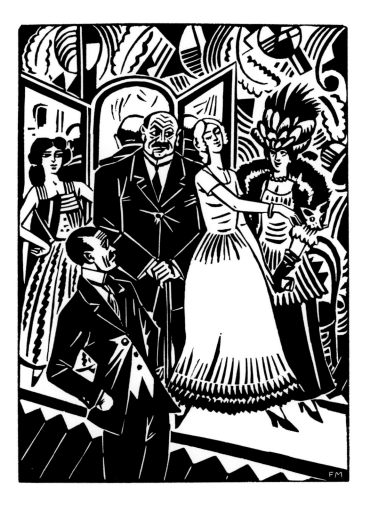

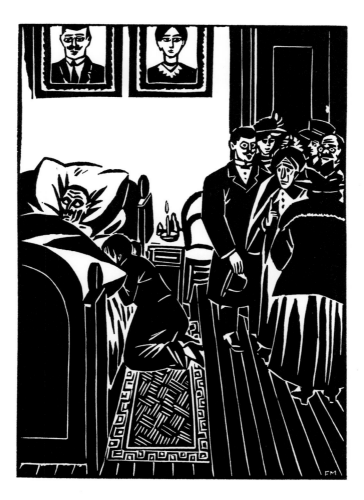

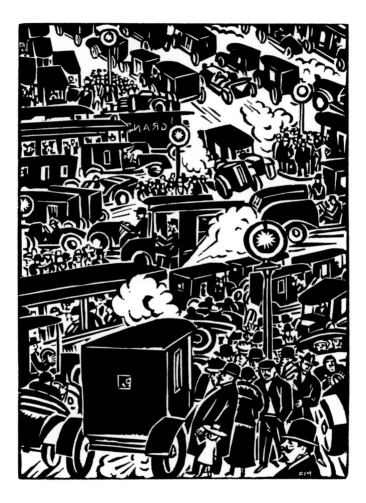

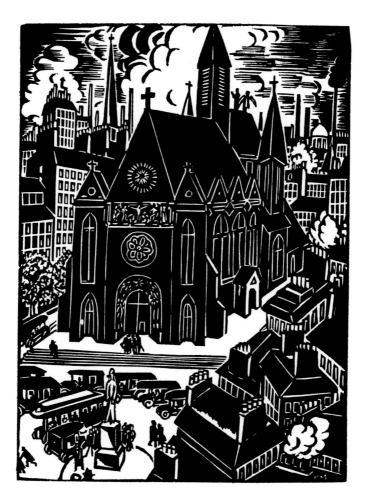

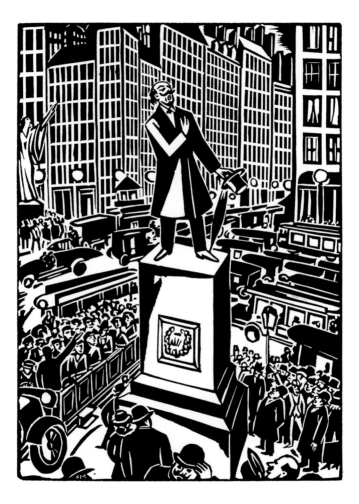

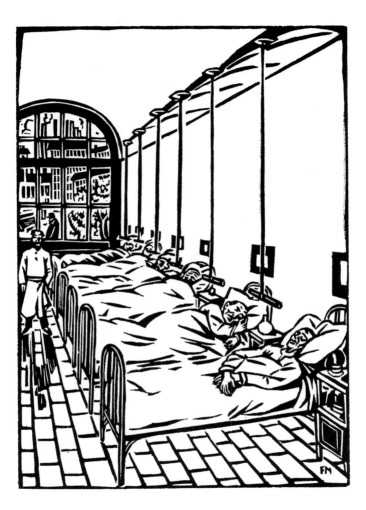

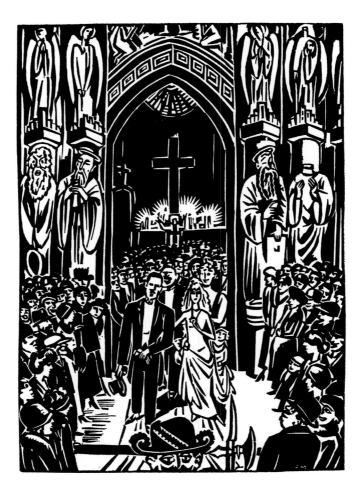

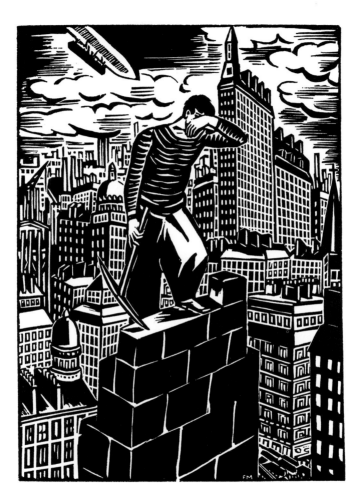

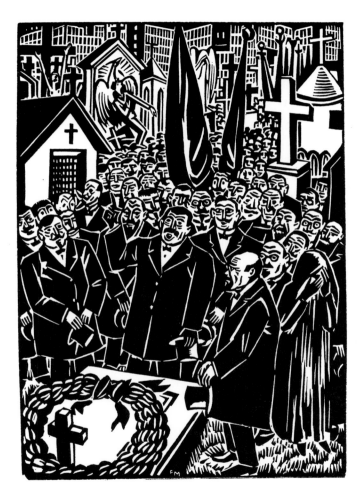

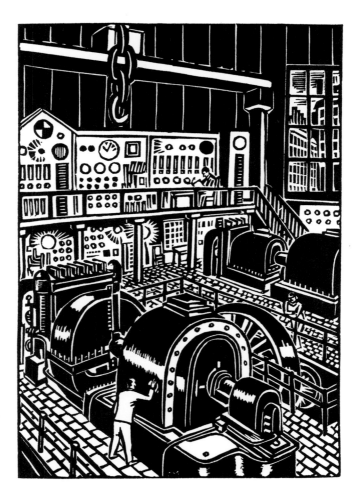

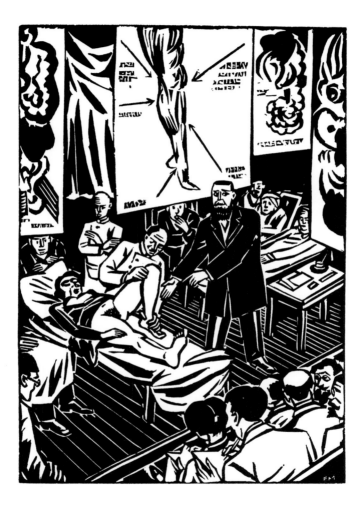

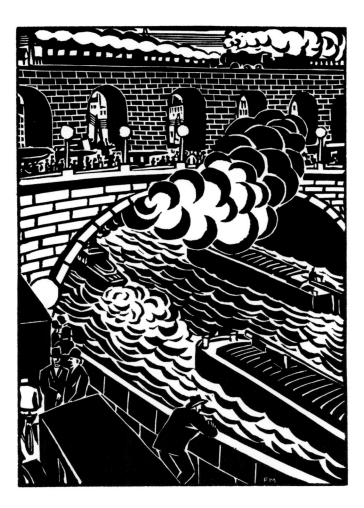

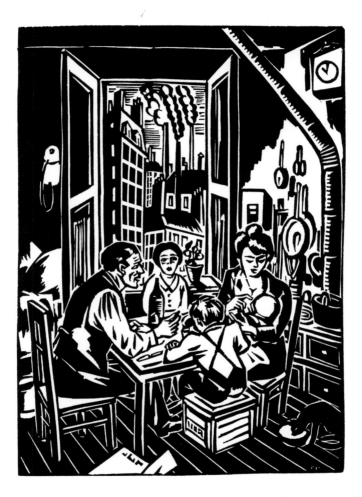

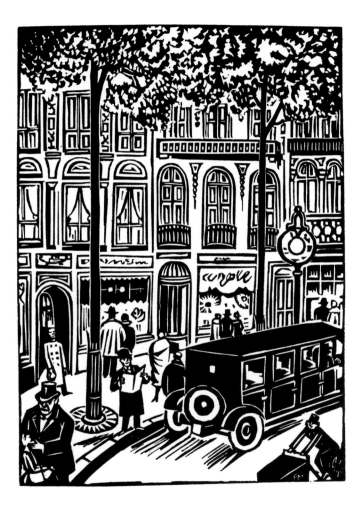

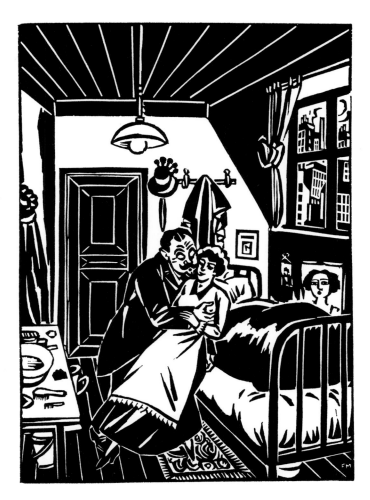

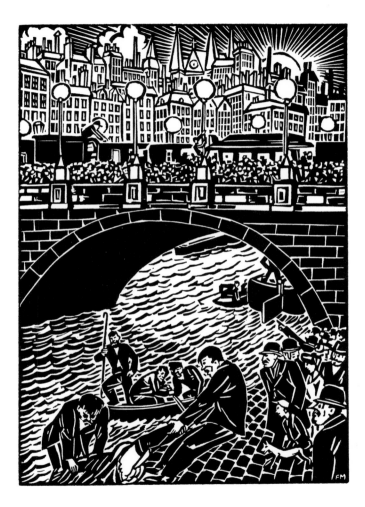

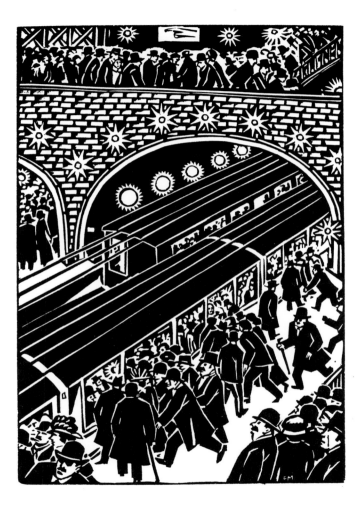

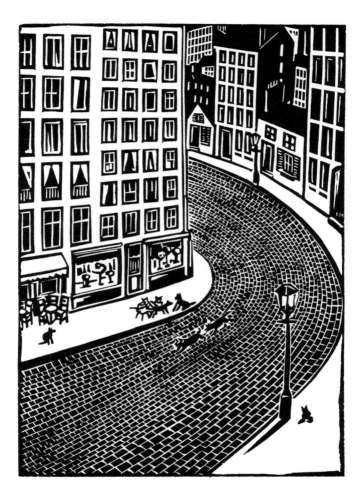

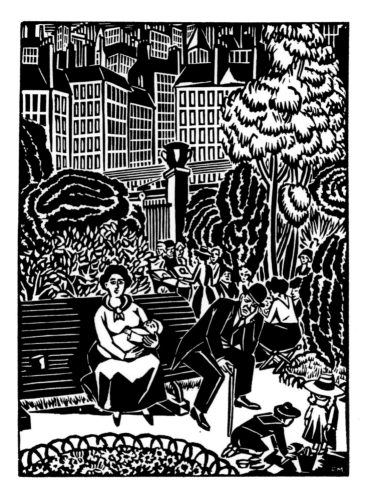

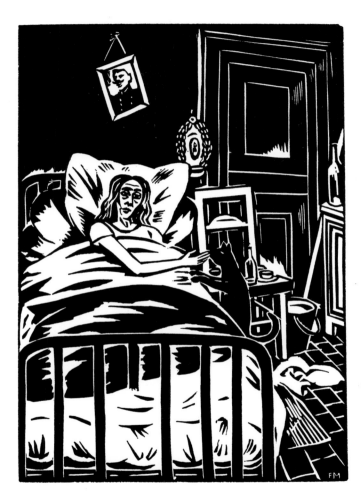

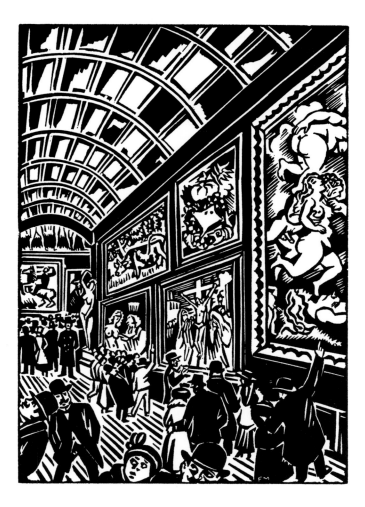

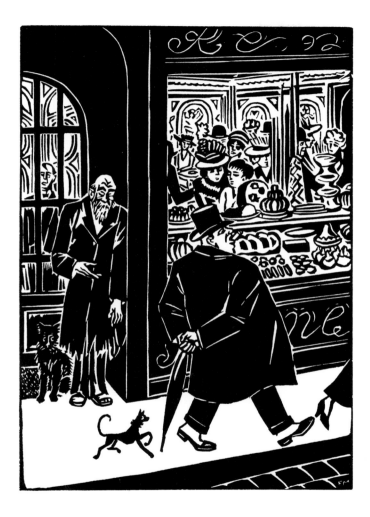

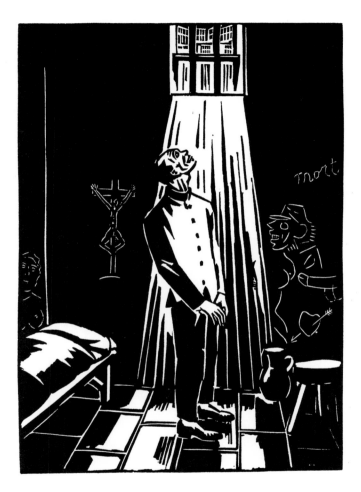

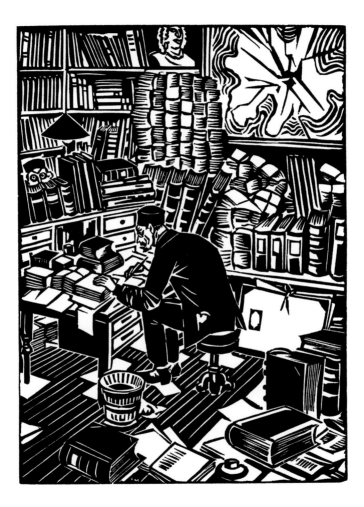

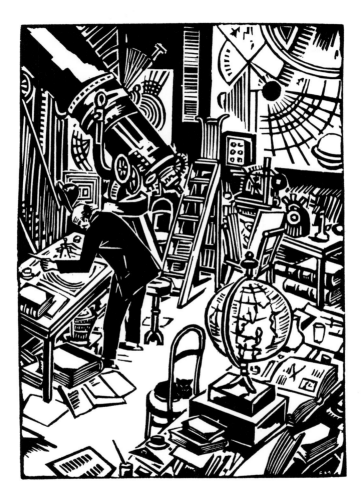

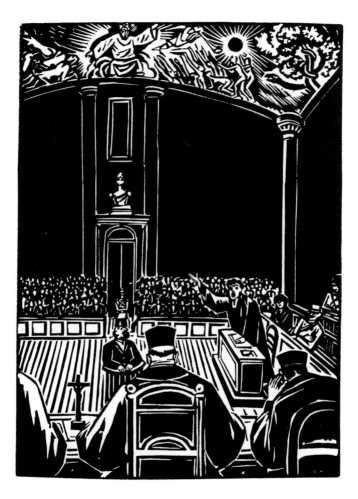

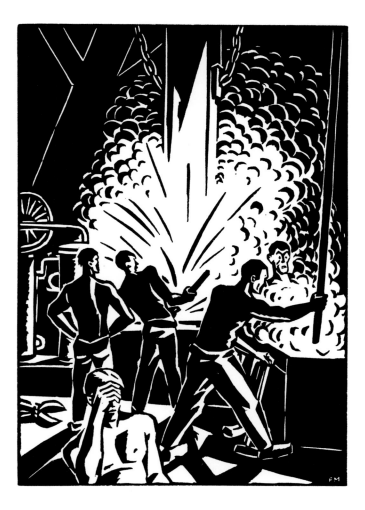

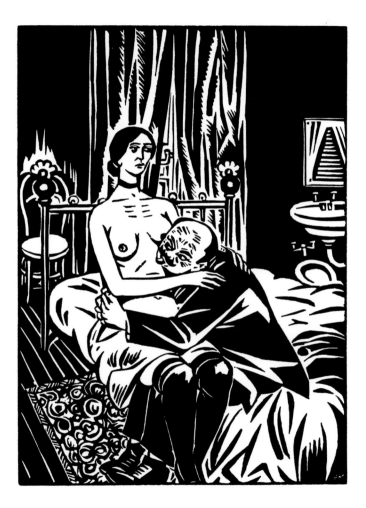

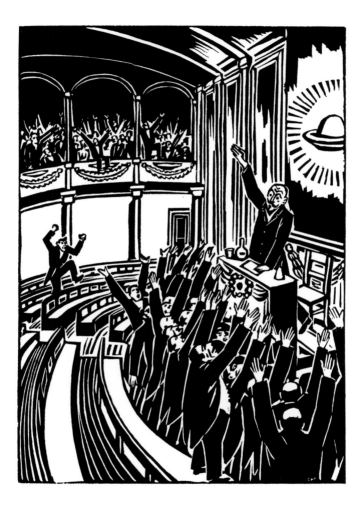

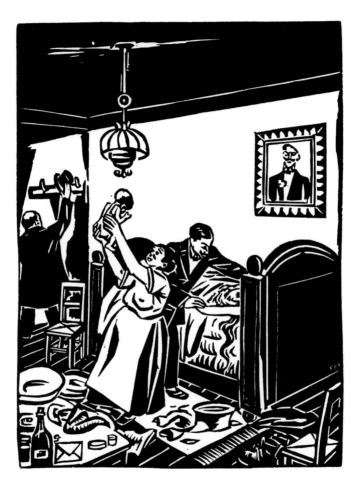

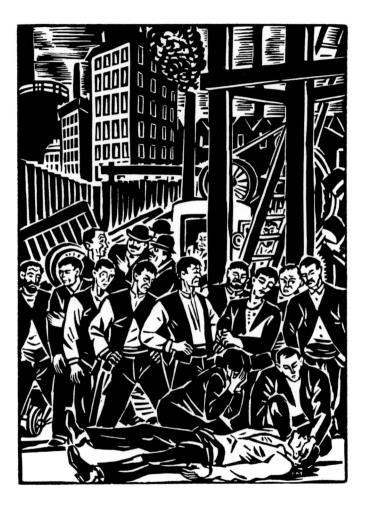

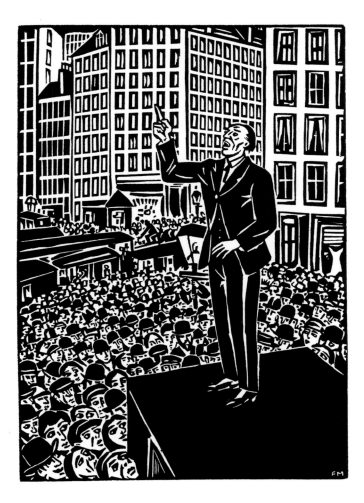

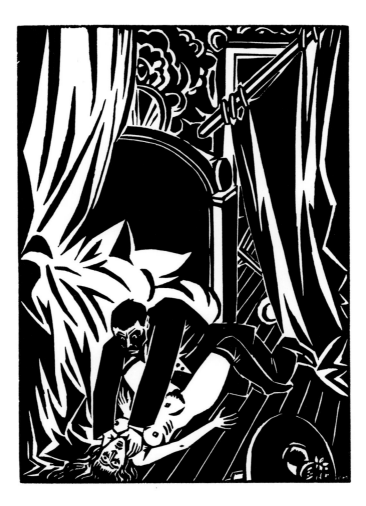

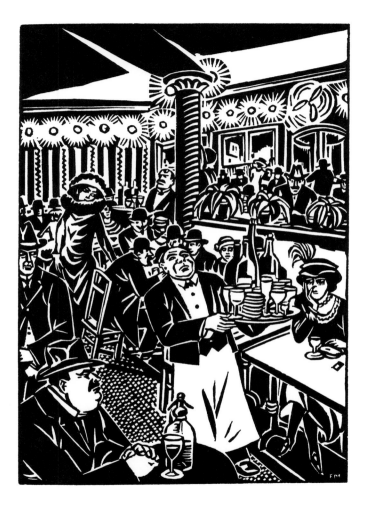

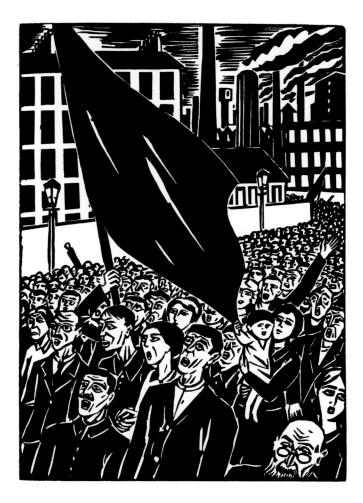

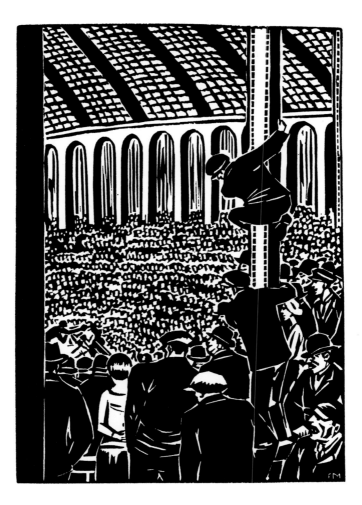

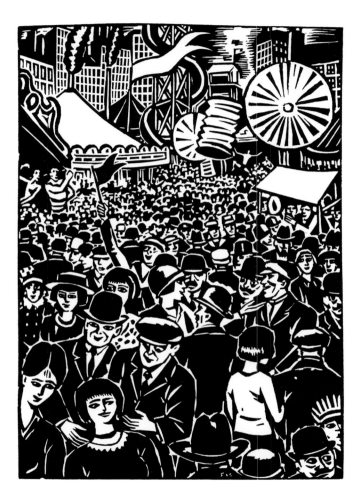

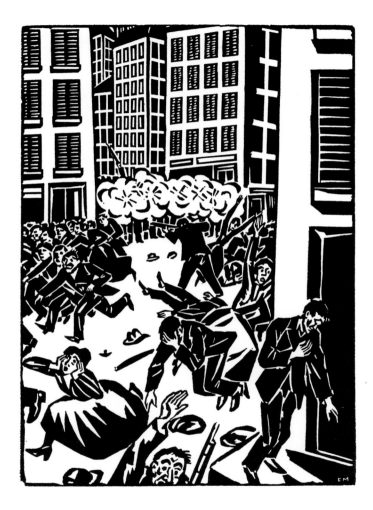

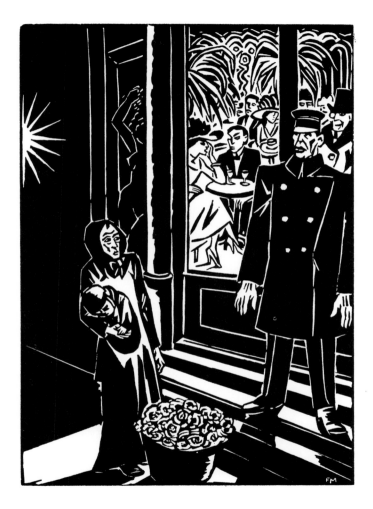

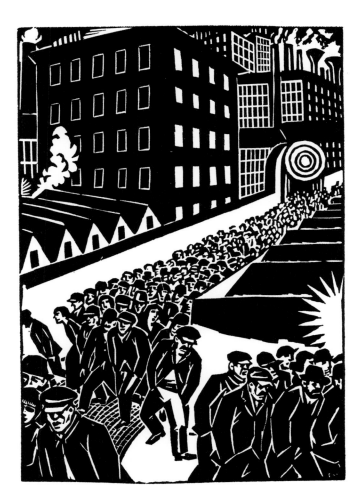

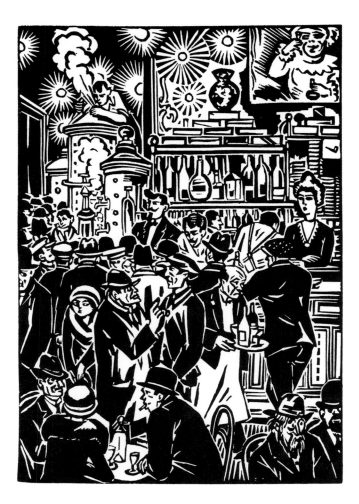

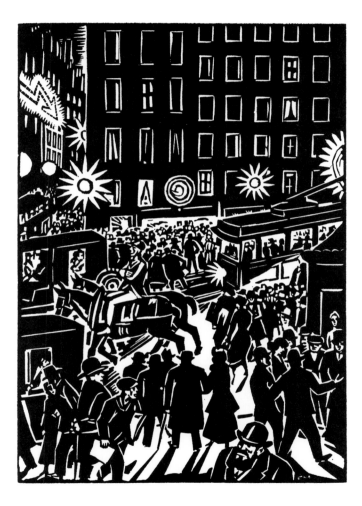

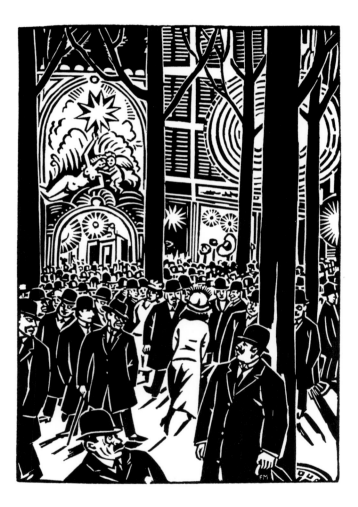

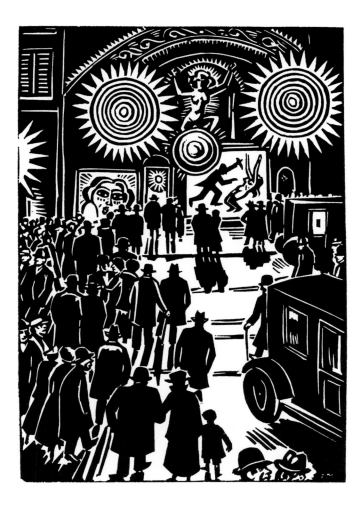

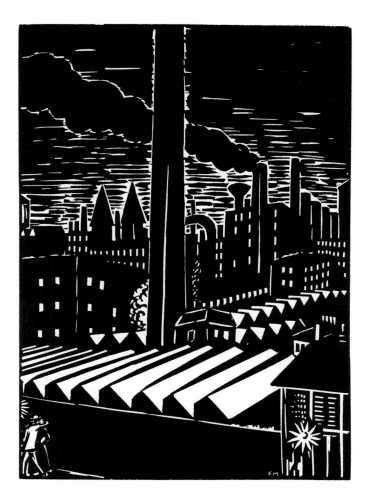

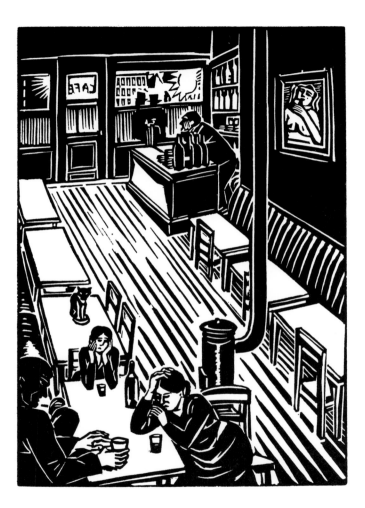

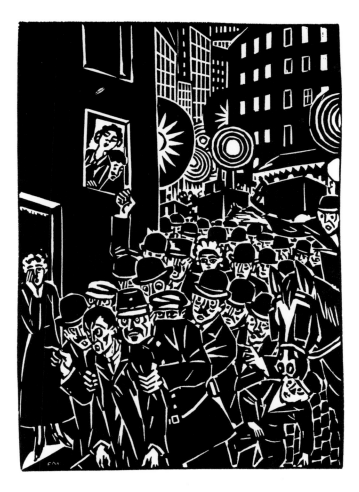

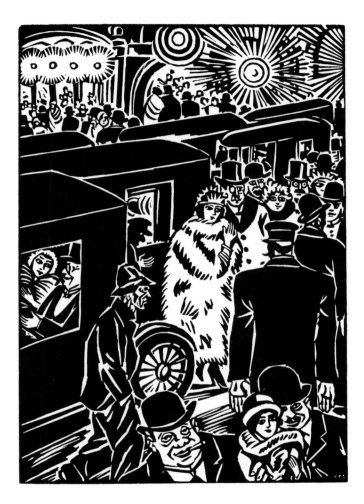

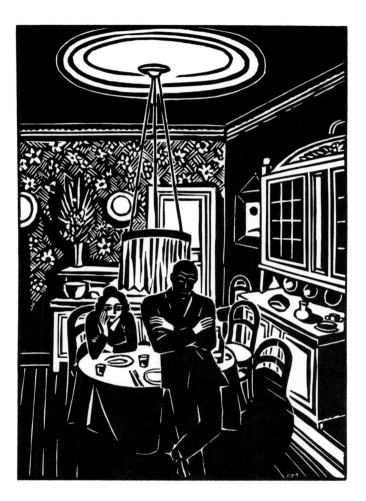

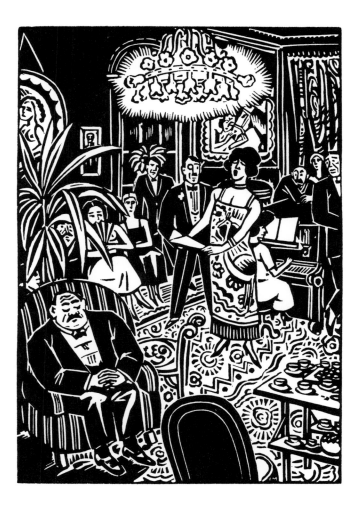

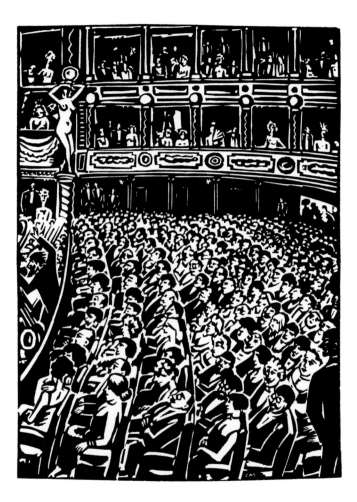

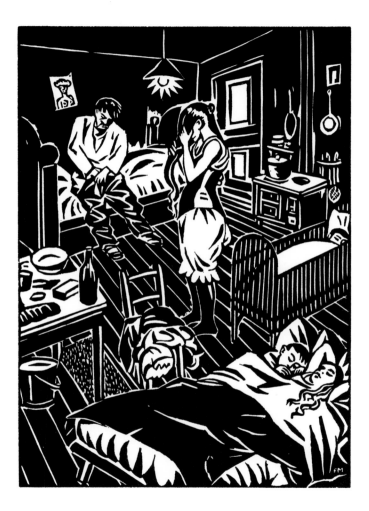

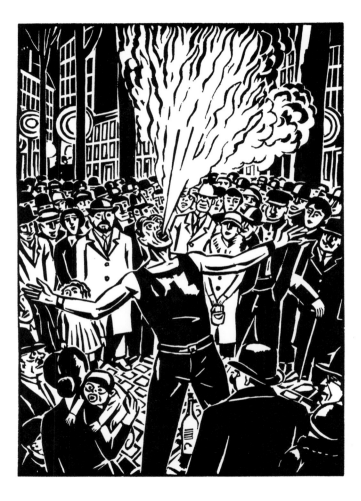

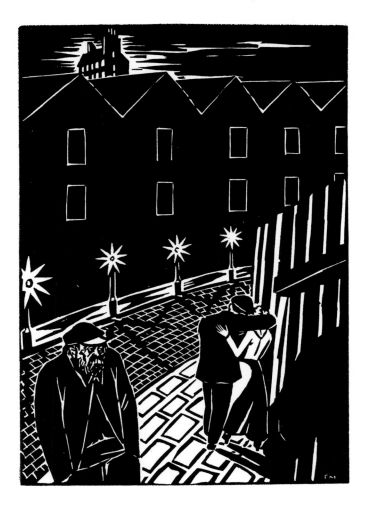

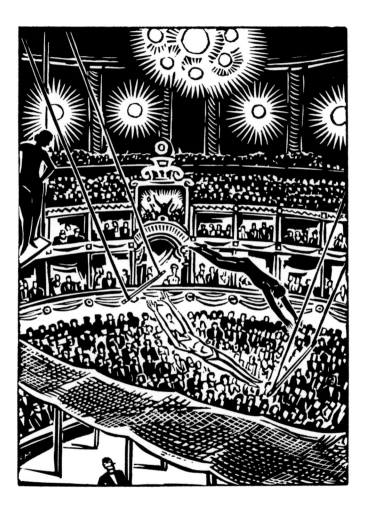

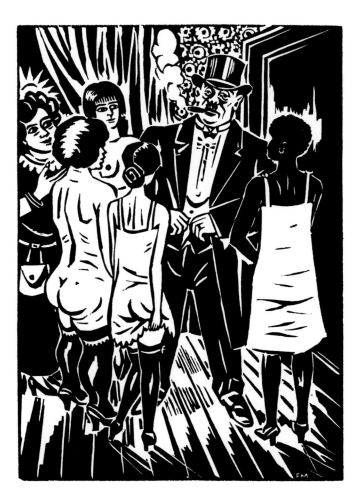

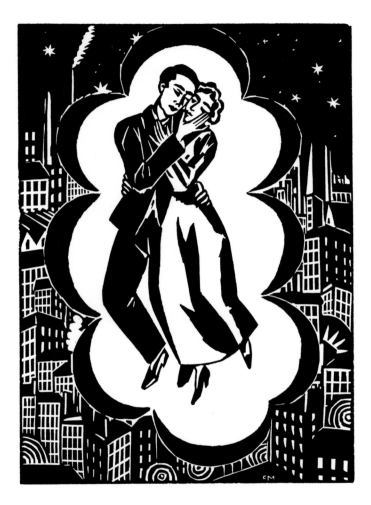

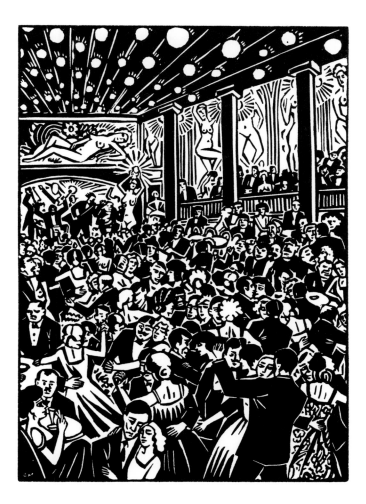

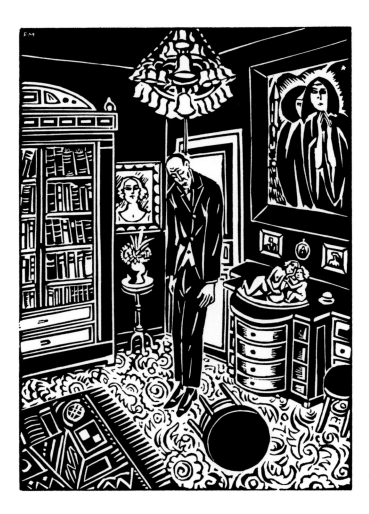

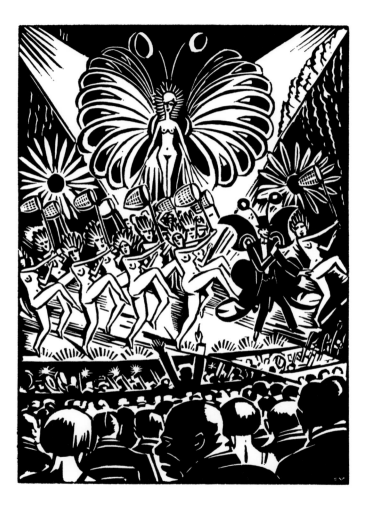

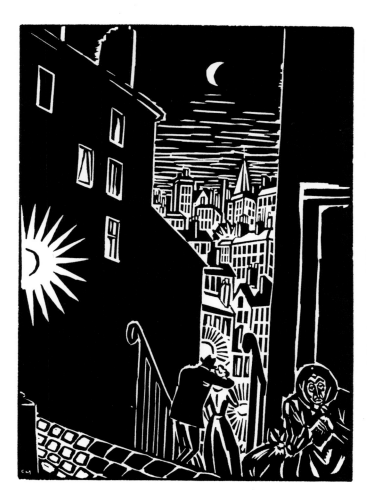

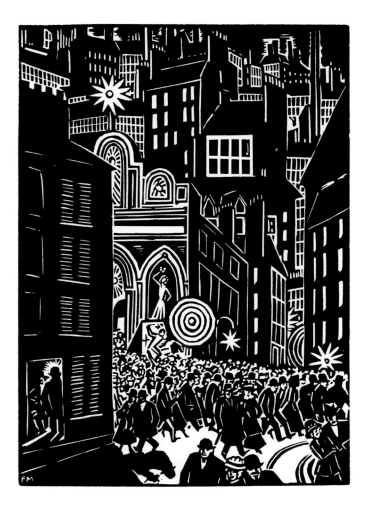

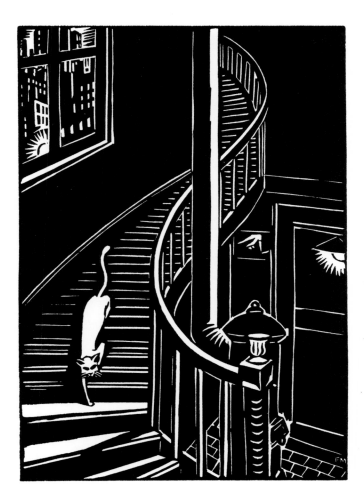

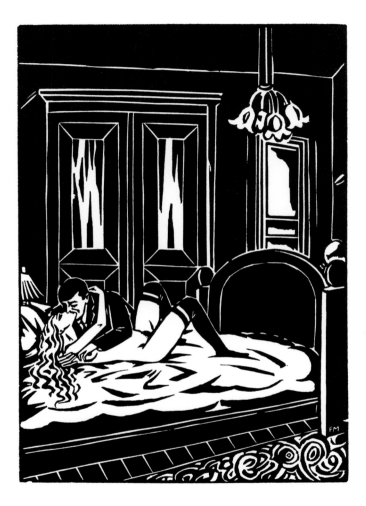

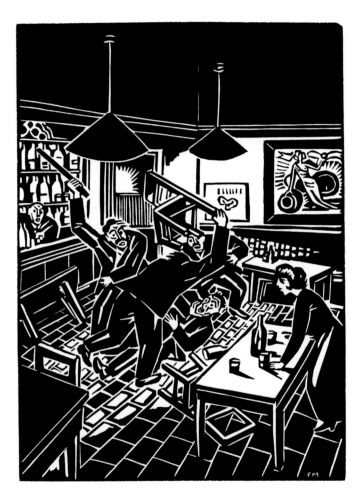

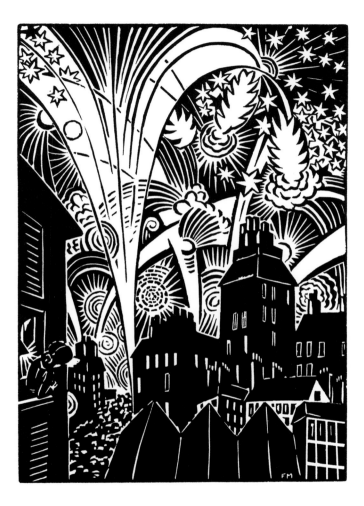

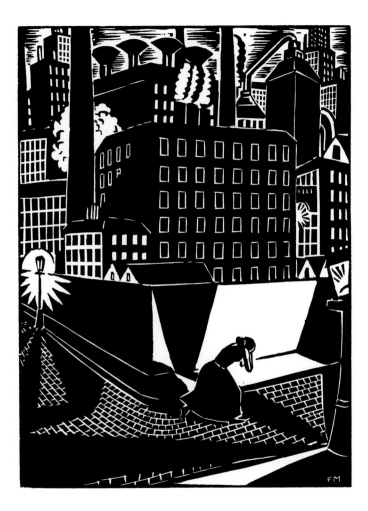

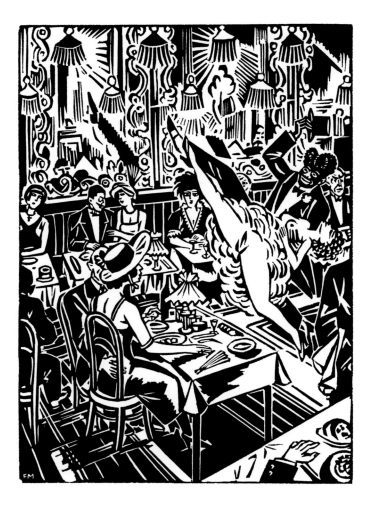

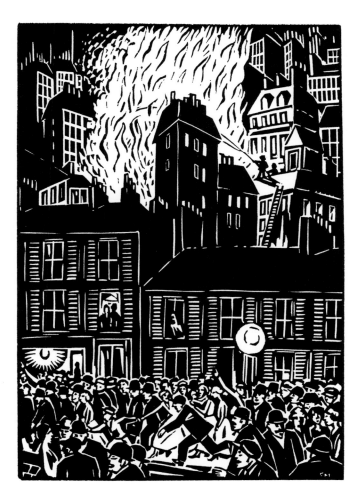

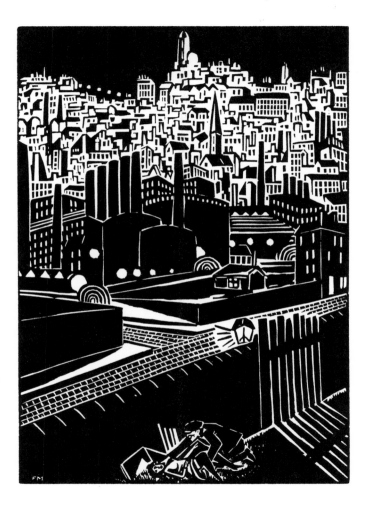

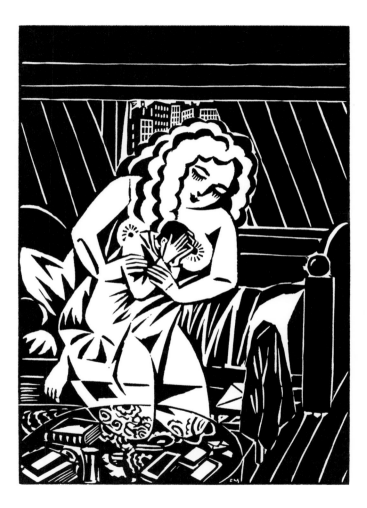

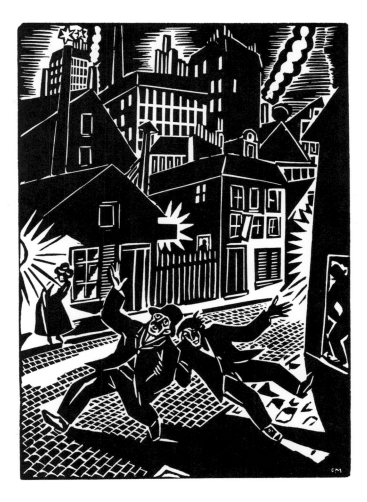

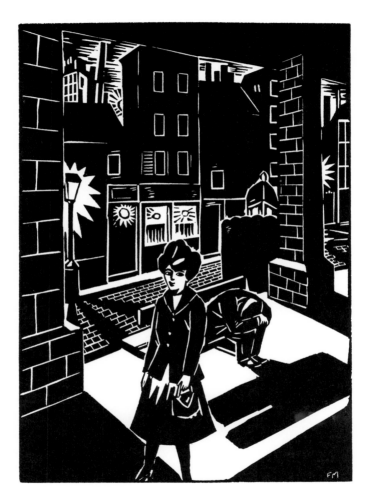

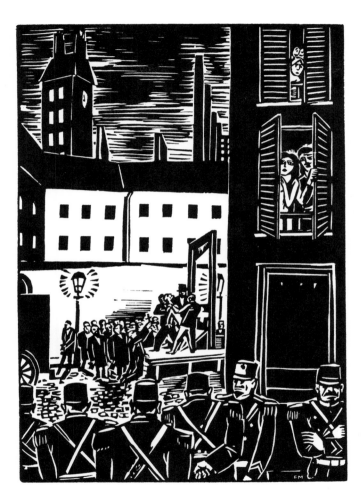

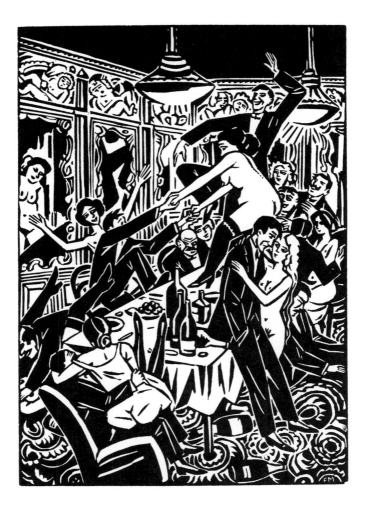

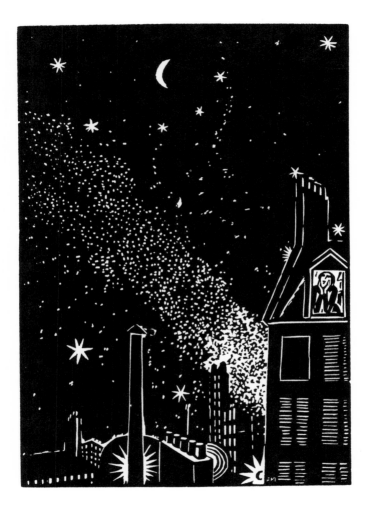

Frans Masereel was born in Blankenberghe, Belgium, in 1889. He spent his youth in Ghent, and the World War I years in Geneva, Switzerland, where, along with Romain Rolland and others, he was active in the anti-war movement. Masereel moved to Paris after the war, and spent time in Berlin and other European cities, associating with such artists as Georg Grosz and Tristan Tzara, and the author Blaise Cendrars, with whom he collaborated.

Masereel had a long association, which lasted through the height of the Expressionist movement, with the German book publisher Kurt Wolff. Inexpensive editions of Masereel's woodcut stories—including *Mein Stundenbuch*, *Geschichte Ohne Worte*, and *Die Stadt*—as well as his illustrations for novels, pamphlets, and posters, made him an extremely popular artist. His work was also published in France, and later in the United States, to great acclaim. In his art and his politics Masereel was always sympathetic to working people and their struggles, and in the late 1920s, artists surveyed by a German magazine named Grosz, Käthe Kollwitz, and Masereel as the most important artists concerned with the daily lives of workers.

During World War II, Masereel moved south from Paris to Free France, where he joined his old publisher and supporter Pierre Vorms, who was active in the Resistance. In 1942, Pantheon Books, in New York, published *Danse Macabre*, a collection of twenty-five drawings that describe the experience of the war. In a letter to the publisher he wrote, "We have lived through tragic days, having left Paris on foot! We have walked for nearly 300 miles, have been bombed and machine-gunned several times a day.... I cannot paint, as there is nothing to paint with. So I am now working out in black and white the sketches which I made during the retreat, or rather the debacle."

After the war he settled in Nice, and continued to produce woodcuts, drawings, and paintings. In 1959 he was invited to China, where the great writer Lu Hsun had overseen publication of several of the woodcut storybooks earlier in the decade, and following the trip Masereel produced a series of paintings and drawings of the modernizing, industrializing nation. A decade later in 1969, at the age of eighty, Masereel was awarded an honorary degree from Humboldt University in East Berlin, and chose the occasion to express his support for the international youth movement and student rebellions.

Masereel died in 1972, in Avignon.